Have You Ever Wondered?

The difference between...

Written and Illustrated by

Katy Lynn Taylor
and
Jeanne Joy Hartnagle-Taylor

Have You Ever Wondered?

ISBN - 13: 978-0-9898800-9-1

BISAC: JNF003000 Juvenile Nonfiction / Animals /

10987654321
Printed in the United States

Table of Contents

Alligator or a Crocodile? **2-3**
Beaver or a Muskrat? **4-5**
Bee or a Wasp? **6-7**
Bison or a Buffalo? **8-9**
Butterfly or a Moth? **10-11**
Camel - Dromedary or a Bactrian? **12-13**
Crow or a Raven? 14-15
Donkey or a Mule? **16-17**
Dolphin or a Porpoise? **18-19**
Duck or a Goose? **20-21**
Elephant - African or an Indian? **22-23**
Frog or a Toad? **24-25**
Mole or a Shrew? **26-27**
Monkey or an Ape? **28-29**
Rabbit or a Hare? **30-31**
Reindeer or a Caribou? **32-33**
Rhinoceros - Black or White? **34-35**
Sea Lion or a Seal? **36-37**
Snail or a Slug? **38-39**
Turtle or a Tortoise? **40-41**

Have you ever seen a winged insect on your windowpane and wondered, “Is that a butterfly or a moth?” Do you know the difference between a frog and a toad? Apes are not to be confused with monkeys, but can you tell them apart?

It is easy to mistake a dolphin for a porpoise because they are alike in many ways. They are closely related animals, but each have their own unique characteristics. Once you recognize the differences it won’t take long to tell which is which. After you read the book, take the quiz on Page 42 to test your animal knowledge.

Alligator or a Crocodile?

Alligators and crocodiles are the largest ***reptiles*** in the world. ***Reptiles*** are cold blooded animals with scales, a backbone and a bony skeleton inside its body. They use lungs to breathe air, but they have no built-in way to control their own body heat. Since alligators and crocodiles rely on the sun for warmth they live in marshlands and jungles where the waters are warm. Like all reptiles, their tough, dry skin is made of overlapping scales. Their olive-green color blends in with their surroundings.

Alligators and crocodiles are agile and aggressive. They can move swiftly on land and in water. They eat fish, birds, turtles and other animals. The young are hatched from eggs their mother lays in nests. Their eyes and nostrils are on top of their muzzle so they can hunt while they hide underwater. It is easy to mistake an alligator for a crocodile. They look very much alike. Both have long, armor-plated bodies, muscular tails and powerful jaws. The best way to tell them apart is to compare their heads. Their snout and teeth are different.

Did you know? The word reptile comes from a word which means to creep. They belly crawl, but can also walk on all four legs. Have you ever heard of crocodile tears? The phrase is used to describe a pretender — someone who cries fake tears of grief. Why do crocodiles cry when they eat? No one knows for sure, but it is believed crocodiles have salt glands near their eyes that produce tears to help their bodies get rid of excess salt.

Alligators	**Crocodiles**
Grayish green color	Tan / green color
Broad and rounded, a U-shaped muzzle	Narrower, a more pointed V shaped muzzle
Pair of large teeth in the lower jaw are hidden when the mouth is closed	Two large teeth in the lower jaw can be seen even when the mouth is closed
Less active	More aggressive

Beaver or a Muskrat?

Beavers and muskrats live in wetlands. They are ***semi-aquatic*** (part water) ***rodents.*** **Rodents** are ***mammals*** (the only group of animals that have fur) with a pair of broad front teeth they use for gnawing. Beavers use their chisel-like teeth to strip bark and cut down trees which they use to build dams. The dams cause an area to flood which creates a pond where they build their lodges. Their homes have underwater entrances.

Did You Know? Beavers provide a safer habitat for muskrats. Muskrats help beavers by eating cattails which opens up paths for beavers to swim through. Beavers use their tails to steer and propel them when swimming (also to slap the water when danger is present).

Beavers	Muskrats
Luxurious, reddish brown fur Wide, flat paddle-shaped tail Usually see only large wedge-shaped head when it swims Adults are two to three feet long Weighs 35 to 60 pounds Powerful, orange-colored, teeth Wide feet five, very distinct toes on front feet Hind feet are webbed Builds lodge in middle of pond using sticks, moss, bark and mud or makes den in river bank Tree bark is their favorite food	Dark brown to black fur Long, flat, skinny rat-like tail Usually see whole body when it is swimming Much smaller - about 12" long Weighs two to five pounds Less powerful white teeth Small feet with four main toes and a tiny 5th toe Hind feet are partially webbed Burrows into river and lake banks or builds nest with a pile of grass on the pond Eats plant life and freshwater mussels

Bee or a Wasp?

Bees and wasps are flying insects with scaly wings. Like all insects, they have six jointed legs, and a three-part body (head, thorax and abdomen). Insects don't have a bony skeleton inside their body, but they have an ***exoskeleton*** (a hard-outside shell). Even though their color is similar bees and wasps act very different. The aggressive Yellow jacket and hornet are types of wasps. Most bees and certain wasps work together in a group called a ***swarm***. Most wasps are less social and do not form groups.

Did You Know? Wasps use their saliva as cement. They chew wood and turn it into paper for building a nest. Bees take nectar in their stomach and change it to honey. When honeybees collect nectar, pollen gets stuck on their furry legs and body and gets rubbed on flowers to pollinate them. Bumblebees make honeypots which look like miniature clay pots. They are slower and gentler than other bees. They also don't lose their stinger after they sting. Stinging insects have bright, vivid yellow and black patterns to warn you - they sting!

Bees	Wasps
Round, furry body with flat, wide legs	Smooth body with tapered waist and round, waxy legs
Visits flowers and sips nectar - *pollinates* (fertilizes) plants	Predator of other insects - eat insect larva and sweet nectar
Builds a geometric wax hive (honeycomb) in hollow logs, tree trunks or man-made boxes	Builds a nest (out of wood pulp or mud) in sheltered places like the eaves of your house
Bees are not aggressive and sting only to protect themselves or their hives when disturbed	Wasps are aggressive and easily annoyed. They will attack without being provoked
Stinger has a barb which they lose after they sting and they die	Don't lose their stinger (not barbed) when they sting - they inject venom

Bison or a Buffalo?

Buffalo are mammals with ***cloven*** hooves. Cloven means the hooves are divided into two toes. They graze grass and other plants as they walk. Their horns never shed off like deer antlers do.

Bison is the Latin name for the American buffalo. They are the largest animals in North America and a symbol of the American West. Bison are an important part of the Native Americans. They depended on them for food, shelter and clothing. They often ate the meat fresh or dried and sometimes mixed it with berries and dried it for long lasting food.

Water buffalo spend much of their day in water. Their hooves keep them from sinking in the mud. The Asian water buffalo has been domesticated since ancient times. They have been used as a draft animal to farm the land and pull heavy loads. The Cape buffalo lives in Africa and has massive horns that form a helmet over its forehead.

Did You Know? Buffalo are ***cud-chewers***. Cud-chewing animals like cows, sheep and goats digest their food in two stages. First, they eat raw plants and grind it into pulp. They regurgitate the cud (partially digested food) and chew it.

Bison	**Buffalo**
Large humped shoulders	No hump
Enormous head with short, sharply pointed horns that curve outward and up	Longer, thick horns that sweep in an outward curve and back toward shoulders
Black beard	No beard
14 pairs of ribs	13 pairs of ribs
Shaggy winter coat that sheds to a lighter summer coat	Short, glossy coat

Butterfly or a Moth?

Butterflies and moths are beautiful, flying insects. Their velvety-looking wings are covered with tiny scales. They are found throughout the world, but there are way more moths than butterflies. Their life history can be told in four words – egg, larva, pupa and adult. Adults lay eggs (about the size of this "o"). Caterpillars hatch out of the eggs which are the larva. Caterpillars eat milkweed leaves and grow. Each time its skin gets too tight, the caterpillar will shed (molts) it and grow larger. This happens several times. As soon as they reach full size, they make a pupa (***chrysalis*** or a ***cocoon)***, a protective covering where the caterpillar goes through a change known as a ***metamorphosis*** to become an adult butterfly or moth.

Did You Know? Butterflies taste with their feet and smell with antennae on their head. Their tongue is a long, flexible tube like a drinking straw for sipping nectar out of flowers. Butterflies and moths ***pollinate*** (fertilize) plants, blossoms and night blooming flowers. Moths use moonlight to help them fly straight which is why they are easily attracted to artificial light. The silkworm is not a worm at all. It is the caterpillar of a moth whose cocoon is made of silk.

Butterflies	Moths
Slender body	Heavier body
Slender antennae with little knobs at end	Feathery or plain antennae, without knobs
At rest - folds its wings upright over their backs	At rest - spreads wings out flat like the wings of an airplane
Usually flutter during the day	Flies mostly at night
Pupa / Chrysalis - hard smooth covering	Pupa / Cocoon - fibrous, silk covering
Some are dull, most have brightly colored wings	Usually dull in color (except a few like Luna moth)

Camel – Dromedary or a Bactrian?

Camels are large mammals adapted to harsh climate of desert, semi-desert, and prairie terrains. They have been domesticated since ancient times. They are used for transportation in the Middle-East. Camels can drink large amounts of water so they can travel long distances in the dry desert without water. They store flesh and fat (not water) in their hump, which can be turned into energy. This allows them to go a long time without water. A large hump is a sign of good health.

They are ***herbivores*** (plant eaters) and feed on grass, leaves and other vegetation. Their tough mouths are able to bite off and chew prickly desert plants. They have wide, thick pads on the soles of their feet with two toes that spread out so they can walk or run without sinking into shifting desert sands. Thick padding on their knee joints protects them against hot, burning sand when they kneel down. Camels can open and close their nostrils to keep dirt and sand out. They also have long eyelashes, broad bones and bushy eyebrows over each eye to protect them from dust during sand storms and to shield their eyes from the bright sun.

Did You Know? Camels are related to Llamas and alpacas. They are known as ships of the desert. The swift Arabian also known as a Dromedary camel is often used as a saddle animal. Camels can live up to 50 years of age. When they are irritated, they spit. They may also bite and kick. The long hair camels shed in the summer is used to make paint brushes and fine cloth.

Dromedary (Arabian) Camels	Bactrian Camels
One hump that forms a sideways "**D**" for Dromedary	Two humps that form a sideways "**B**" for Bactrian
Long legs	Shorter body, heavier legs
Short hair - lives in Northern Arabia, Africa and India well adapted to the Sahara Desert	Longer, shaggy coat - well adapted to cold winters on the rocky deserts of Central and East Asia

Crow or a Raven?

Crows and ravens are jet-black birds with glossy feathers. Birds are the only class of animals with feathers. Crows and ravens are perching birds with strong legs for walking. They are also acrobatic fliers. They have four-toed feet (three toes pointing forward and one pointing backward). Sometimes they steal bright metal objects and hide them. Their nests are built with sticks and twigs and lined with softer material like grass, bark and moss. Crows do not usually migrate with the changing seasons. They feed on vegetables, fruit and seeds and meat. They also love corn and steal eggs. When a group of crows known as a ***murder*** of crows is eating, there are usually one or two sentinels as lookouts for danger while the others eat.

Did You Know? Ravens are intelligent and highly adaptive. They've been known to speak in captivity. When the prophet Elijah was hiding by the brook Cherith in Jordan, God commanded the ravens to feed him. They would take him bread and meat every morning and evening. –***First Book of Kings* 17: 1-6** in the Old Testament in the Bible.

Crows	Ravens
Smaller - about 17 to 19 inches tall	Large- can get to 26 - 27 inches tall
Flatter bill - looks sleek and neat at rest	Curved bill w/tufts of plumage (shaggy throat at rest)
Rounder, blunter tipped wings Squarish, fan-shaped tail	Longer, pointed wings / Wedge, diamond-shaped tail
Shrill voice "caw caw caw"	Deep, croak, "gronk gronk"
Outgoing - scavenges in a group	***Scavenges*** or hunts alone
Two dozen different calls	20 to 100 different calls
Lives up to about eight years	Live as long as 30 years
Builds nest in tall trees	Builds nest high in treetops or on top a rocky cliff

Donkey or a Mule?

Donkeys are related to horses and zebras. They were domesticated by in Africa long before the horse. Donkeys are smaller than horses and generally live longer than horses (from about 25 to 50 years). The donkey has long been known as a draft animal to carry heavy loads. Like the horse, donkeys are mammals with hoofed feet. They have a single, solid hoof on each foot.

Mules are the offspring of donkeys and horses. They are more surefooted than horses and often used for carrying packs, and for riding on steep mountain trails. Mules and donkeys are herbivores and spend most their day grazing grass. They sleep standing up. When they feel safe, they sometimes sleep while lying down.

Did You Know? The Spanish name for donkey is burro. A **f**emale Donkey is called a Jenny and a female mule is a Molly. The donkey is also known as an ***ass,*** which comes from its scientific name, *Equus* ***asinus***. This is also why the male donkey is sometimes called a jackass.

Donkeys	Mules
Size of a pony about four feet tall at shoulder	Taller / resembles a horse
Long ears	Shorter, horse-shaped ears
Tuft of hair on tip of tail	Tail is more like a horse
Mane is shorter, and stiffer	Sleeker main and tail
Bray – hee haw	Whinny, but then a bray
Can reproduce offspring - has 62 chromosomes	Sterile (cannot reproduce offspring) - 63 chromosomes
Less intelligent, less trainable and less stamina	More intelligent, more obedient, more stamina

Dolphin or a Porpoise?

Dolphins and porpoises are playful sea creatures. They live in the ocean, but they are not fish. They are marine ***mammals*** (warm-blooded animals that breathe air and nurse their young on milk). Dolphins and porpoises breathe through a blow hole on the top of their head. Their jaws are lined with pointed teeth they use for catching fish. The melon in their forehead is used to ***echolocate*** (bounce sounds off objects) to locate prey when hunting.

Did You Know? Dolphins are some of the fastest animals in the ocean. They swim by moving their tail up and down. The orca (also known as the killer whale) is the largest type of dolphin. Dolphins work together to hunt for prey. They circle a ***school*** (group) of fish and swim closer and closer to herd them into a tight ball to keep them from escaping.

Dolphins	Porpoises
Larger / leaner and sleeker in appearance	Smaller, stouter and more compact in appearance
Between 4 to 30 feet	Between 4 to 8 feet
Fin – curved like a wave	Triangular fin (like a shark's fin)
Elongated jaws, pointed beak-like nose	Flatter face, blunt jaws, no beak
Uses its blow hole to communicate under water	Does not communicate under the water
Friendly – interact with humans and swim in the wakes of ships	Shyer – does not swim alongside boats
Jump clear out of the water	Rarely leap out of the water
Talkative and makes sounds able to be heard	Sounds unable to be heard by the human ear
Travels in large schools	Travels in small schools

Duck or a Goose?

Ducks and geese are ***waterfowl*** (water birds) and live in wetlands on ponds and lakes. They have webbed feet for swimming, but they can also walk on land. They are ***omnivores***, animals that forage on all sorts of food including grass, seeds, grains, insects; and fish, snails and slugs. Ducks and geese have soft, downy (fluffy) feathers under their outer feathers to keep them warm. They keep their outer feathers oiled by preening them with oil from oil sacs which grow near their tails. There are both wild and tame ducks and geese. Wild ducks and geese migrate, flying in groups to different climates as the seasons change. They make their nests in a simple depression in the ground and line it with grass, leaves and feathers.

Did You Know? The downy feathers from ducks and geese are used for insulating clothing and bedding. ***The Ugly Duckling*** by Hans Christian Andersen is a story about a homely little bird that everyone made fun of until he matured. Much to his delight (and the surprise of the others), he was actually a beautiful and graceful swan (a cousin to ducks and geese). Swans have 23 bones in their neck. A duck has only 16 bones in their neck. Birds have more bones in their neck than a giraffe. Can you imagine that? A giraffe has only seven bones in its neck.

Ducks	Geese
Stouter with a shorter neck	Larger with elongated neck
Large, flat bills	Pointed bill
Short legs	Longer legs
Waddle as they walk - feet are usually farther back on their bodies	Walk better than ducks - Legs are nearer the middle of their bodies
Hens make a quacking sound	Honks and hisses
Dive for underwater plants and small fish	Graze grass and dip their heads under water for food

Elephants – African or an Indian?

Elephants are the largest land animals on earth. They live in family groups and form very strong social bonds. They eat grass, leaves, tree bark and bananas. Their feet are cushioned with pads of elastic muscles. Elephants use their ears to fan air over their body. Their trunk is a long nose. They breathe through two nostrils at the end it. The little knobs at the tip of the trunk are used like fingers to pick up objects like a blade of grass. They also use their trunks to trumpet, to lift trees, move things to get food, or to carry heavy loads. Elephants love to bathe in water, but they don't drink water through their trunk. They suck water into their trunk and then squirt it into their mouth or spray it over their body.

Did You Know? Elephant are excellent swimmers. Their ***tusks*** are large pointed ivory teeth. They live wild on the grassy plains of Africa or in the rain forest in Southern Asia. The females are called cows. Males are called bulls.

African Elephants	Indian Elephants
Larger and heavier	Shorter, stockier
Huge, floppy ears	Smaller ears
One dome on forehead	Two domes on forehead
Skin is more wrinkled	Skin is less wrinkled
Lower lip is short and round	Lower lip is long and tapered
Slightly hollowed back	Arched back
Tallest point the shoulders	Tallest point is on the back
Two knobs at the tip of trunk	One knob at the tip of its' trunk
Four nails on front feet and only three nails on the hind feet	Five nails on front feet, four nails on the hind feet
Difficult to train	Domesticated - easily trained

Frog or a Toad?

Frogs and toads are amphibians without tails. ***Amphibians*** are cold-blooded animals like reptiles, so their temperature varies with the weather. Amphibians are different from reptiles because they don't have scales. Amphibian means double and life or living in two places. During the first stage of life, ***tadpoles***, also known as ***polliwogs*** are hatched from eggs the adults lay in water. Tadpoles swim using a tail and they breathe with gills like fish. Before long, their tails fall off as their legs grow and they develop lungs for breathing air.

To keep cool, frogs absorb water through skin on their belly and legs. That's why they sit on moist ground or in the water. Their long, sticky tongue is useful for catching flies and other insects. Their bulging eyes let them see in front, to the sides and towards the back a little bit. They make croaking sounds by forcing air from their lungs through their vocal cords.

Did You Know? A group of frogs is called an army. Toads and frogs may have a 30 to 40-year life span. In cold winters, frogs can burrow in the mud to ***hibernate*** (go into a deep sleep). In hot, dry climates of the desert they bury themselves in the sand to escape the heat. Frogs can breathe through their skin.

Frogs	**Toads**
Body with longer hind legs	Short, compact body and shorter hind legs
Good jumpers – they leap	Poor jumpers – they hop
Smooth, moist skin	Dry, bumpy skin
Webbed hind feet	Hind feet not webbed
Large bulging eyes	Eyes are more recessed
Always lives close to water – lives on land less than toads do	Land-dwelling / can live in the desert as long as there is enough water to lay their eggs

Mole or a Shrew?

Moles and shrews are among the smallest of the true mammals. They are burrowing creatures. They dig extensive tunnels, like an underground highway system. Their soft, velvety fur insulates them against extreme temperatures.

Moles and shrews are always hungry. They are ***insectivores*** (insect eaters) not rodents like mice. They have five clawed toes on their feet (mice have four toes). Their eyesight is poorly developed, but they have very sensitive whiskers on their face with long, flexible snouts.

Did You Know? A newborn shrew is shorter than a teaspoon, but an adult is only a few inches long. Moleskin is such a luxurious fur it was used to make stylish clothes in the 19th century. The type of moleskin used to treat a blister is not moleskin at all, but a cotton adhesive fabric.

Moles	Shrews
Larger	Smaller – mouse-like
Flexible, hairless snout	Long, pointed snout
Very tiny ears and eyes – poor hearing and virtually blind (but can detect light from dark	Small eyes and ears - poor vision, but excellent senses of smell and hearing
White tipped teeth	Reddish-brown tipped teeth
Broad, shovel shaped front feet with long claws – small, narrow hind feet	Small mouse-like feet
Live beneath the soil in underground tunnels they excavate (dig)	Live mostly in woodlands - they make runways through dried leaves and grass in forest floor
Eats insects, insect larvae (white grubs) and earthworms	Eats insects, snails, slugs, worms and mice

Monkey or an Ape?

Apes and monkeys are ***primates***, the highest order of animals. Primates live in a variety of habitats from hot tropical jungles, dry grasslands to mountain and rain forests. Monkeys and apes have flexible fingers and toes like we do which enables them to pick up food and small objects with no trouble. Chimpanzees poke sticks into termite mounds to catch insects for food. Apes and monkeys are very good tree climbers. They often live in trees and can easily move from tree to tree. All primates, except full-grown Gorillas can climb trees. Gorillas are too heavy to swing from vines. The Chimpanzee, Gibbon, Gorilla, and Orangutan are types of apes and are found only in Africa and Asia. Monkeys are divided into two groups, Old World and New World. New World monkeys such as the Capuchin, Spider Monkey the Howler are from South and Central America. Old World monkeys like the Baboon, Mandrill and the Rhesus Monkey are found in Africa, Asia and Europe. Primates hunt mainly plants, fruits, nuts; insects. Some eat small animals.

Did you know? Primates, especially monkeys are very social creatures. A group of monkeys is called a troop. Primates were created on the sixth day along with the other land animals, but they are not as high as man. Man was created in God's own image - ***Book of Genesis*** 1: 26-27.

Monkeys	Apes
Arms are same length or shorter than their legs	Arms longer than their legs – walk more upright
Smaller head and body with slender, long chest	Larger head and body with a broad back
Tails - New World monkeys have ***prehensile*** (tails that curl around branches and grasp them). Old World Monkeys don't have prehensile tails, but they have pads on their rumps.	No tails Highly intelligent - capable of learning sign languages, uses tools and displays problem solving skills

Rabbit or a Hare?

Rabbits and hares belong to the same family, but they are different. Both have long ears and strong hind legs for hopping and digging. They have short tails and communicate danger by thumping their feet on the ground. Rabbits and hares are ***nocturnal*** (night-time) creatures. They eat grass and other plants.

Did You Know? A colony of rabbits can dig many tunnels in a bank. The Cottontail is a type of rabbit and the Jackrabbit is a type of hare. Some hares are able to hop up to 40 miles per hour (64 km) and leap up to 10 feet (3 meters). Have you ever heard the phrase "Mad as a March Hare?" During the spring, hares can be seen chasing each other around meadows during daylight. ***The Tale of Peter Rabbit*** by Beatrix Potter is a delightful children's story about the adventure of a mischievous and disobedient young rabbit as he is chased through Mr. McGregor's vegetable garden.

Rabbits	Hares
Smaller and not as fast	Larger and swifter
Shorter ears	Longer ears
Shorter legs with smaller feet	Longer legs with larger feet
Nests underground in ***warrens*** or burrows connected by tunnels	Nests on surface in shallow hollow on the ground and among meadow grass
Gregarious - lives in groups	More solitary
Born helpless – unable to see and without fur	Young are born fully furred and able to see
44 chromosomes	48 chromosomes
Female is called a doe; the male is a buck and a young rabbit is called a kitten or bunny	Young hare is called a leveret

Reindeer or a Caribou?

Reindeer are large arctic deer that have been domesticated for many centuries by the ***Sami*** from the northern parts of Norway, Sweden, Finland and the ***Nenets*** of the Siberian arctic in Russia. These nomadic reindeer herders use them for milk, meat, and clothing and for transportation. Caribou are wild reindeer. The native ***Inuit*** people of the far north in Alaska and Canada hunt caribou for food, clothing and shelter. Their antlers and bones are shaped into tools and toys.

Caribou survive harsh winters by ***migrating*** (travelling) between the ***tundra*** (treeless plains) to forested areas. Unlike other types of deer, both male and female reindeer and caribou have antlers. They use their antlers and their sharp-edged hooves to scrape through the snow for food. Their shovel-shaped hooves are wide so they can easily walk in snow and paddle through rushing water. Their footpads become soft in the summer for walking across the spongy, wet tundra. Arctic deer eat Reindeer moss, a type of ***lichen*** (fungus and algae) that sprouts up through the snow. When the weather warms up they eat grasses, willow shoots, moss and mushrooms.

Everyone has heard the popular Christmas story about ***Rudolph, the Red-Nosed Reindeer*** and how he saved Christmas. **Did You Know?** All reindeer have special noses that warm the air before it is inhaled into their lungs. They can run between 37 and 50 miles per hour and they are strong swimmers. The hair in their thick overcoat is hollow and traps air to insulate against freezing temperatures. It also helps keep them from sinking when swimming in icy cold water.

Reindeer	Caribou
Smaller, shorter legs, stouter and slower	Larger, longer legs, slimmer and faster
Flatter, dish-shaped face	Roman-nose (prominent bridge)
Brownish summer coat – whitens in winter (even spotted)	Dark summer coat - light winter coat – no spots

Rhinoceros – Black or White?

Rhinoceros have a huge body with a broad chest and a short neck. Their large head has two horns projecting from the snout. They are the second biggest hoofed mammal on earth. Rhinos have three toes on each foot. The word rhinoceros is from a Greek word, ***rhino*** meaning nose and ***ceros*** meaning horn. Their habitat ranges from ***savannahs*** (grasslands) to dense forests of Africa and Asia. They graze on grass or eat leaves and twigs. Rhinos look clumsy, but they can wheel around and charge at speeds of up to 30 miles per hour. They are well-known for their poor eyesight, but they have a very strong sense of hearing and smell.

Did you know? There are five types of Rhinoceros. Black and White Rhinos come from Africa. The main difference between a black rhino and a white rhino **is not the color at all,** but the shape of their upper lip. No one knows how White Rhinos got their name, but many think it comes from an African or Dutch word which meant ***wide*** to describe the shape of their mouth. There are also Indian, Javan, and the hairy Sumatran Rhinoceros. The Indian Rhino (also known as the Greater One-Horned Rhino) is large like the White Rhino, but has only a single horn on its' nose. They have thick, folded skin that looks like a suit of armor.

Black Rhinoceros	White Rhinoceros
Pointed lip for plucking twigs and leaves from shrubs and trees	Flat broad mouth (wide upper lip) grazes grass on the ground like a cow
Usually dark brown in color and only half as heavy	Light gray larger with a prominent hump
Very aggressive	More docile
Smaller front horn above the nose	Front horn above the nose larger than back
More solitary – travels alone	Gathers in small herds

Seal or a Sea Lion?

Sea lions and seals are fun-loving marine mammals. They live mostly in water, but they breathe air. They also spend time on land and ice basking in the sunlight. They are somewhat awkward on land, but they are expert swimmers. They are as much at home in the water as the fish they hunt. Their rounded, streamlined bodies glide through the water easily. They almost seem to fly. They can swim fast for short distances, even on their backs. Sea lions and seals have a thick layer of blubber that insulates them in ice cold water to keep them warm. They are fish-eaters.

Did You Know? They belong to the wing or fin footed family (along with the walrus). A group of seals is called a colony. Males are known as bulls; females are cows and baby sea lions are pups.

Seals	Sea Lions
Rarely perform	Known as performing seals
Chubby, small head with short, thicker neck	Larger head with longer, more flexible neck
No flaps - have earholes	Small earflaps (pinnae)
Shorter front flippers with fur	Long front flippers without fur
Wavy whiskers	Long, smooth whiskers
Less outgoing	Outgoing – congregate in large groups on land
Quieter, makes soft grunts	Noisy – barks and grunts
Swims by using back flippers like a fish tail	Swims by using front flippers like bird wings
On land they wiggle and pull their body forward using only their front flippers	Flexible hind flippers. On land – they walk on all four flippers

Snail or a Slug?

Snails and slugs are a type of ***mollusk*** (soft-bodied animal without a backbone). They are related to other mollusks such as the clam and oyster, except snails and slugs are ***gastropods*** (belly-footed). Land snails slink along on their long, muscular foot by contracting muscles under their body. They make a type of wave, leaving silver trails of slime which creates a smooth, slippery surface to glide along.

Snail's bodies are either light gray, black, tan or dark green with or without spots or other patterns. They have two pairs of feelers called ***tentacles.*** Their eyes are at the tips of the longer, more slender tentacles. These light sensitive tentacles are also used to smell. The shorter tentacles are used for touch and taste. The snail's soft body is protected by a hard shell they crawl inside to keep predators out and moisture in. Slugs are like snails, but without external shells. Instead, they have a shell-like plate inside their body protecting their breathing cavity. They breathe through an opening or air hole on the side of their body. They also absorb oxygen through their moist skin so they must live in damp places.

Snails and slugs feed on leaves. They damage healthy, living plants by eating them with their raspy tongue like a file which has thousands of teeth like scales. They also eat fungus and decaying vegetation. They are a source of food to birds, fish, frogs and waterfowl.

Did You Know? Snails (and slugs) can actually glide across a piece or glass or a razor blade without being cut. Have you ever heard, "Move at a snail's pace?" Snails creep along slowly at a rate of about ten feet per hour. ***The Snail and the Rose Tree*** by Hans Christian Andersen is a fairy tale about an idle snail who sits beneath a blooming, simple-minded rose tree. His shell contains a great deal – that is, himself.

Snail	Slug
Coiled body which can be drawn completely into its spiral shell	No outside shell Straight body

Turtle or a Tortoise?

Turtles are the only reptiles with shells. The turtle's shell is made of hard, bony scales (like your fingernails) which is part of its skeleton. When in danger, most turtles can withdraw their head, legs and tail into their shell which protects them. Soft-shelled turtles have a leathery covering instead of scales. You can tell whether a turtle lives mostly on land or in the water by the shape of its shell. Land dwelling turtles spend about equal time on land and water. Turtles that live in woodlands along marshes, streams and rivers are known as ***Terrapin.*** They breathe air, even if they live in water. Turtles have no teeth, but their jaws are razor sharp. The tortoise and other turtles eat a wide variety of plants and fruit. Some turtles are *omnivores* (eat plants and animals such as fish and ducklings). All turtles lay their eggs on land. When baby turtles are hatched, they head for nearby water.

Did You Know? *The Hare and Tortoise* is an *Aesop's Fable* where a hare made fun of a slow-moving tortoise. The hare challenged him to race. The hare said, "Don't be silly, I can run circles around you and still win. The hare took off and quickly passed the tortoise. He laughed at the tortoise's slow pace. The hare was so confident of winning the race he took a nap midway. The tortoise kept moving along. He quietly passed the napping hare, but he didn't stop to rest. When the foolish hare woke up he didn't see the tortoise anywhere so he ran as fast as he could go to the finish line. When he got there, he found it was too late. The tortoise had already won the race. The theme of the story is: Slow and steady wins the race!

Turtles (Terrapin)	Tortoises
Dwell near water	Terrestrial (land-dwelling)
The shell is flatter and more streamlined	The shell is heavier, higher and more dome-shaped
Some have slightly webbed feet	Sturdy, short feet with bent legs
Eyes, nearer the top of the head	Eyes focused downward and toward objects in front of them

Is the picture on page 02 - **Alligators or a Crocodiles?**
Is the picture on page 04 - **Beaver or a Muskrat?**
Is the picture on page 06 - **Bees or Wasps?**
Is the picture on the bottom of page 08 **- Bison or a Buffalo?**
Is the picture on page 10 - **Butterflies or Moths?**
What type of Camel is pictured on the top of page 12 – **A Dromedary or Bactrian camel?**
Is the picture on page 14 - **Crow or a Raven?**
Is the picture on the bottom of page 16 - **Donkey or a Mule?**
Is the picture on page 18 - **Dolphin or a Porpoise?**
Is the picture on page 20 - **Duck or a Goose?**
Is the picture on page 22 - **African or an Indian Elephant?**
Is the picture on page 24 - **Frog or a Toad?**
Is the picture on the bottom of page 26 - **Mole or a Shrew?**
Are the animals pictured on page 28 - **Monkeys or Apes?**
Is the picture on page 30 - **Rabbit or a Hare?**
Is the picture on page 32 - **Reindeer or a Caribou?**
Is the picture on page 34 - **What Kind of Rhinoceros?**
Is the picture on page 36 - **Seal or a Sea Lion?**
Is the picture on the top of Page 38 - **Snail or a Slug?**
Is the picture on the top of Page 40 – **Turtle or a Tortoise?**

ANSWERS:

Picture on Page 2 - **A *congregation* (group) of crocodiles.**
Picture on Page 4 - **A Beaver.**
Picture on Page 6 - **Bees.**
Picture on Page 8 – **An Asian Buffalo.**
Picture on Page 10 - **Moths.**
Picture on Page 12 - **A Dromedary Camel is pictured on top.**
Picture on Page 14 - **A Crow on the bottom.**
Picture on the bottom of Page 16 - **A Mule.**
Picture on Page 18 - **A Dolphin.**
Picture on Page 20 - **Geese.**
Picture on Page 22 - **An Indian Elephant.**
Picture on Page 24 - **Frogs.**
Picture on Page 26 - **A Mole.**
Picture on Page 28 - **Apes – An Orangutan on the ground and a Gibbon is pictured in the tree.**
Picture on Page 30 - **A Hare on top and in the middle / A Rabbit on the bottom.**
Picture on Page 32 - **A Reindeer.**
Picture on Page 34 - **An Indian Rhinoceros.**
Picture on Page 36 – **Seal Lions.**
Picture on Page 38 – **A Snail on top.**
Picture on Page 40 - **A Tortoise on the top.**

ABOUT THE AUTHORS

Katy Lynn Taylor is a young author and illustrator whose been drawing pictures and writing stories since she was little girl. ***Have You Ever Wondered?*** is her first published work co-authored with her mother, Jeanne Joy Hartnagle-Taylor.

Jeanne Joy is the author of several books including *All About Aussies: The Australian Shepherd from A to Z, All About Aussies: The Complete Australian Shepherd, Greasepaint Matadors and Stockdog Savvy.*

www.ingramcontent.com/pod-product-compliance
Lightning Source LLC
LaVergne TN
LVHW052300100826
845147LV00001B/105